Revitalize, Recharge, Refocus

Regaining Your Career Momentum

Table of Contents

Chapter 1. Introduction

Dive into a captivating and uplifting journey of self-discovery and professional growth with our Special Report "Revitalize, Recharge, Refocus: Regaining Your Career Momentum". This power-packed guide will embark you on a thrilling voyage, recapturing your lost workplace zest, re-energizing your motivation, and realigning your professional direction towards soaring heights. Tailored with expert insights, inspiring success stories, and actionable strategies, this report is your trajectory planning companion - the spark to rekindle your career with confidence and vigor. Ready to reignite your work life, amplify productivity, and achieve unthinkable career pinnacles? Let this Special Report be the first step in your revitalizing journey. Hold on tight. Your breakout awaits!

Chapter 2. Revitalizing your Career: The Essential Kickoff

"Revitalizing your career goes hand-in-hand with personal revitalization: the two are intertwined. Only by developing the self can one truly envision and steer the course of change and progression in their professional journey.

2.1. Understanding The Need for Revitalization

Often, we find ourselves feeling passionless, unmotivational, or simply stuck in our current career paths. This can be a product of numerous factors – unrewarding work, lack of growth opportunities, or an uncertain career trajectory. Understanding that the need for revitalization extends beyond extricurricular dissatisfaction to your very psyche is essential. A lack of motivation or passion for your work can negatively impact your mental and emotional health, disrupt your personal life, and leave you feeling lost and unfulfilled.

2.2. Identifying Your Personal And Professional Needs

Start by taking a comprehensive assessment of what you desire from your career. This will help you establish a foundation on which you can plot your improved trajectory. This is a three-step process:

1. Purpose: Reflect on what truly matters to you. What are you passionate about? What brings you joy and satisfaction? What do you fundamentally value?

2. Skills: Evaluate your core strengths and weaknesses. What makes

you unique in your field of work? What areas can you improve, and how can you leverage these skills to their fullest potential?

3. Alignment: How well do your current role and organization align with your purpose and skills? Are you in a position that allows you to express your passion and exercise your strengths?

Each of these steps will provide you with a better understanding of where you currently stand and where you wish to head.

2.3. The Mindset Shift: From Passivity to Proactivity

The first pivotal step towards revitalizing one's career lies within adopting a proactive mindset. Transitioning from a passive participant in your professional life to an active architect of your journey is critical. This shift starts with harboring the notion that change is possible — and it starts with you.

2.4. Developing A Strategic Plan

A strategic approach is necessary to propel your career in the desired direction. This begins with establishing a clear vision of what success looks like to you. Developing SMART (Specific, Measurable, Achievable, Relevant, Time-bound) goals can accelerate your progress and maintain ongoing motivation. Enumerate your goals, both short-term and long-term, keeping them relevant to your defined purpose and skills.

2.5. Embrace Lifelong Learning

One of the most transformative ways to revitalize your career is through continual learning. The learning curve in the job industry has steepened over the past decade, consistently placing a premium on up-to-date knowledge and skills. Embrace this trend by actively seeking opportunities:

1. Professional Courses: Whether it's through online platforms or professional workshops, new skills relevant to your field are always at your disposal.

2. Networking: Regularly connect with professionals in your field. Gain insights into current industry trends, new technologies, future forecasts and development opportunities.

3. Books and Podcasts: Educate yourself on leadership, emotional intelligence, communication, and other soft skills that supplement your technical skills.

2.6. Practice Resilience: Overcoming Setbacks

During your revitalization journey, obstacles and setbacks are bound to occur. Practicing resilience in these situations is paramount. Each failure should be viewed as an opportunity to grow and learn, rather than as a deterrent. This perspective can be achieved by cultivating a growth mindset, viewing challenges as opportunities rather than obstacles.

In conclusion, career revitalization begins with you and ends with the achievements that you envision for yourself. The journey may be filled with challenges and detours, but every step taken is a step towards building the career of your dreams. Let your passion fuel you, your resilience guide you, and your vision lead you. Are you ready to take the plunge?"

This concludes the process of revitalization. We will delve into how to recharge your motivation in the next chapter.

Chapter 3. Recharging through Rediscovery: The Power of Your Inner Strengths

Starting on a journey of career revitalization may initially seem like a daunting leap into the unknown. Yet it's key to understand that the power to recharge dwells not in the external world but within us. It lies in our inner strengths - the unique blend of innate qualities, learned skills, and life-acquired wisdom that makes us who we are. And a rediscovery of these strengths can be invigorating, often acting as the necessary push towards recharged professional vigor.

3.1. Identifying Your Inner Strengths

The first pivotal step in tapping into your inner strength is identifying it. Each one of us is power-packed with unique capabilities and a distinct set of strengths. Recognizing them allows us to better utilize them in the pursuit of our career objectives.

To get started, conduct a thorough self-assessment by making a holistic list of your strengths. Consider the full spectrum of your skills - not just technical aptitudes, but also your personal traits, productivity methods, and problem-solving approaches. Reflect on your past experiences and achievements. What skills did you utilize most effectively to succeed in those situations?

Use the SWOT (Strengths, Weaknesses, Opportunities, Threats) analysis technique to plunge deeper into your introspection. Mapping out your strengths and weaknesses, along with the external opportunities and threats, can yield valuable insights into your inner strengths.

3.2. Building on Your Strengths

Identified strengths are like raw diamonds; they can glitter far more impressively when polished and honed. Building on your strengths implies directed efforts towards mastery. The more adept you become in your areas of strength, the more you maximize your productivity and performance.

Determine how you can further leverage your strengths at work. Does your communication proficiency allow you to excel in team collaboration? Can your analytical competency help you deliver high-quality projects? Think about ways in which you can capitalize on your strengths within your current role.

Seek feedback from your colleagues, supervisors, or mentors. Their inputs can provide precious external perspectives on areas you can improve, furnishing your strength-development plan.

3.3. The Power of Mindfulness

Mindfulness is a potent tool for harnessing your inner strengths. It involves cultivating awareness about the present moment - your thoughts, feelings, and circumstances - without any judgment. Mindfulness broadens your ability to recognize your strengths and tune in to your values and goals.

Incorporate mindfulness practices, such as meditation and mindful breathing, into your daily routine. They can reduce stress, boost emotional intelligence, and promote well-focused, thoughtful actions.

3.4. Leveraging Strengths in Goal Setting

Your strengths can significantly influence your goal setting. By aligning your objectives with your strengths, you can create a synergistic effect that fuels your motivation and amplifies your success rate.

Break down your larger career objectives into achievable, strength-focused milestones. This process provides a sense of direction and a clear roadmap leading towards your longer-term goals.

To add a layer of accountability, consider sharing your goals with a trusted colleague or mentor. Their support and guidance could prove invaluable as you journey towards your professional aspirations.

3.5. Fostering Resilience

Resilience - the ability to bounce back from failure, is a core inner strength. It is the power that aids you in maintaining persistence, fortitude, and a positive attitude in face of adversity.

Consider previous setbacks you've overcome and identify the resilience-fostering skills used. Then, nurture these skills through activities such as maintaining a growth mindset, practicing self-compassion, and seeking support when required.

Combining resilience with the perpetual development of your other inner strengths equips you with a versatile arsenal. You not only power through challenging situations but also grow professionally and personally over time.

Identifying, building, and leveraging your inner strengths can recharge your professional life in an extraordinary way. Trust in your capabilities, refine them, and allow them to guide your career path. A rediscovery of your inner strengths not only revives your dwindling workplace zest but also sets you on an upward professional trajectory. Remember that the journey of career revitalization, while challenging, can be deeply rewarding - an opportunity to shape your professional destiny. Embrace it with courage and enthusiasm. For within you lies the power to transform your career. The journey has only just begun!

Chapter 4. Refocusing: Carving out Your Unique Professional Path

Professional growth and success don't accidentally stumble into our lives; they are the yield of meticulously planned and pursued career paths. These paths are unique, etched with our individual skills, dreams, and potential, illuminating the road our professional journey is destined to tread. However, often in the hustle-bustle of the mundane, we lose sight of this trail, leading to stagnation and a decline in motivation levels. Refocusing is your compass helping you recapture your wayward professional course, and in this section, we will guide you on how to unveil your unique professional lane.

4.1. Discovering Your Core

Your first step to refocusing is self-discovery. Comprehending your passions, strengths, weaknesses, values, and career interests is vital. Having an understanding of the 'self' can act as that lens, focusing your professional course as per the defined persona.

Start with conducting a SWOT analysis of yourself, identifying your Strengths, Weaknesses, Opportunities, and Threats in your current professional scenario. Note these down meticulously as they will serve as the background for your future career strategies. Combine this with the introspection of your dreams and ambitions. What do you see yourself achieving in the long run? Visualize your ideal workplace, your role, your achievements. This amalgamation of introspective self-analysis and forward-looking vision is the foundation upon which your unique professional path will be drawn.

4.2. Prioritizing Goals

Post discovering your core, the next step is to establish your career goals. What is that you ultimately desire to accomplish in your professional life? But remember, these goals must align with your core to maintain a consistent trajectory.

Set both short-term and long-term goals. Short-term goals would comprise immediate targets, for instance, learning a new skill or getting a certification that could enhance your professional value. On the other hand, long-term goals represent the broader picture of where you foresee your career aligned with your vision for yourself.

Bear in mind, these goals should be SMART: Specific, Measurable, Achievable, Relevant, and Time-Bounded. Such goals are more effective and motivate you to stay focused and committed in your pursuit.

4.3. Deconstructing Goals into Actionable Milestones

Remember, your goals are not to be achieved overnight. They require gradual, consistent effort. Therefore, breaking them into smaller, manageable milestones makes the trajectory easier to tread.

For every goal, create sub-goals. For instance, if your objective is to learn a new skill, break it down into: identifying the skill you want to grasp, finding a course/mentor for it, scheduling a timeline for learning, and implementing it in your work. This approach makes your goals less daunting and more achievable, boosting your motivation and ensuring continued focus towards your end-goal.

4.4. Embracing Continuous Learning

The dynamism of the professional world mandates constant learning and adaptability. To stay relevant and competitive, we need to persistently upgrade ourselves, acquire in-demand skills, and align with industry trends.

Commit to developing a learning culture around you. Whether it is through books, online courses, webinars, or workshops, institutionalize a habit of continuous learning. This habit not only broadens our perspectives but also keeping us engaged, motivated, and in line with our professional path.

4.5. Cultivating Resilience

Roadblocks, failures, and rejections are inevitable parts of any journey. It is through resilience you can stay steadfast on your path, forging ahead remorselessly despite what comes your way.

Cultivate an attitude of resilience. Celebrate your wins, learn from your losses. Don't get disheartened by dead-ends, rather see them as an opportunity to re-route. Each failure is a lesson that paves your unique professional path further and makes your journey richer.

4.6. Networking and Mentorship

Building your professional network and finding a mentor can be transformative in charting your professional course. A good network opens up avenues for collaborations, insights, opportunities while a mentor guides you with their wisdom and experience.

Volunteer for industry events, participate in webinars and networking platforms, connect with professionals on social media. Concurrently, find a mentor who aligns with your career path and can guide you through their expertise and experiences. They not only help you navigate through your professional journey but also instill confidence in your self-growth and achievements.

Refocusing requires persistent effort, introspection, and an unyielding commitment to your goals. It's a journey where you architect your unique professional path with indomitable passion and unwavering focus. It's about rekindling your inner spark and shining on the path that leads you to the unprecedented pinnacles of professional success. Embrace this journey with courage and serenity for your breakout awaits! Your voyage into the world of refocus starts now. The destination? A revitalized, invigorated you. Bon voyage!

Chapter 5. Constructive Self-Evaluation: Unveiling Your Authentic Career Aspirations

Constructive self-evaluation is an integral part of any professional growth. It is the baseline assessment, the very foundation from where the edifice of renewed, revitalized career aspirations is erected. It is the mirror held up to your professional self, reflecting your strengths, outlining areas for improvement, and highlighting hidden capabilities that can edge you ahead on your career pathway.

5.1. Establishing Your Self-Evaluation Foundation

To initiate the self-evaluation process, sit in solitude, free from distractions. Quiet moments spent with yourself are often the source of breakthrough insights. Close your eyes, take a deep breath, and reflect on your professional journey so far. Dive deep into your experiences, analyzing moments of triumph as well as those riddled with challenges and failures.

Once you've gathered your thoughts, create four sections titled: Strengths, Weaknesses, Opportunities, and Threats (SWOT). Start populating each section by brainstorming thoughts related to your professional life.

The 'Strengths' section includes your skills, talents, and abilities that make you unique in your profession. The 'Weaknesses' section outlines areas you struggle with, or where you lack knowledge or expertise. The 'Opportunities' section underscores the possibilities for growth within your current role or industry, whereas 'Threats' highlights potential hindrances or challenges in your path to success.

Strengths	Weaknesses	Opportunities	Threats
Skillset A	Weakness B	Current market trends favoring your skills	Emerging technology making your skill obsolete
Expertise C	Knowledge gap D	Openings for leadership roles	Economic downturn
Personal attribute E	Personal challenge F	Networking opportunities	Intense competition

5.2. Understanding Your Personality Type

It is equally important to understand your personality in terms of work preferences and behavioral traits. Personality assessments like the Myers-Briggs Type Indicator (MBTI) can offer profound insights. Remember, acquiring self-knowledge is not about fitting into labels. It's about understanding your unique wiring - how you think, feel, react, and behave in different workplace scenarios.

5.3. Setting Authentic Career Aspirations

This step involves aligning your professional goals with your authentic self. Go back to your SWOT analysis. Which strengths align with your career aspirations? Which weaknesses can hamper your growth? Which opportunities do you need to seize? Which threats should you beware of?

Write down your aspirations and the steps needed to achieve them, breaking down large goals into actionable milestones. Use SMART goal methodology – Specific, Measurable, Achievable, Relevant, and

Time-Bound. That brings clarity and eases the execution process.

SMART Goals	Actions Steps
Goal 1: Specific, Measurable, Achievable, Relevant, Time-Bound	Action step 1, Action step 2, Action step 3
Goal 2: Specific, Measurable, Achievable, Relevant, Time-Bound	Action step 1, Action step 2, Action step 3

5.4. Breaking Your Self-Limiting Beliefs

Break free from untrue beliefs that confine your potential. It's human to fear failure, but it is also human to prevail despite fear. Unpick your self-limiting beliefs by recognizing them and challenging their validity. If you see yourself shackled by a "cannot do" or a "not good enough" mindset, ask - Is it really true? Or is it a belief stopping you from tasting success?

5.5. Seeking Constructive Feedback

Lastly, seeking feedback can be a great addition to self-evaluation. It offers an external perspective that may unveil new viewpoints about your career performance. Reach out to your colleagues, supervisors, or mentors for honest, constructive feedback.

Through a comprehensive understanding of your skills and gaps, preferences and peculiarities, goals and inhibitions, constructive self-evaluation provides a solid foundation for career revitalization. Use this knowledge as your roadmap, propelling you forward toward achieving your aspirations, as you continue in your quest for professional growth and betterment.

Chapter 6. Rolling with the Punches: Embracing Change in the Workplace

The contemporary work environment is dynamic, continually evolving in response to myriad factors such as technological advancements, the economic landscape, demographic alterations, and societal shifts, to name a few. Navigating this tumultuously transforming environment necessitates a degree of adaptability, an ability to adjust one's sails in headwinds. Embracing change is no longer an optional trait; it is an indispensable survival skill in today's workplace.

6.1. Recognizing the Nature of Change

Change, in its many shapes and forms, is an inevitable aspect of life and, by extension, our professional sphere. Whether it's a transition to a new role, a shift in the company's direction, a novel technology introduction, or an economic downturn that mandates layoffs, the employment landscape is in a constant state of flux. Despite being unavoidable, the dread of change chock-full of uncertainties frequently instills a sense of fear and distress in employees.

Active recognition of change as a natural occurrence, however, eases the associated anxieties, enabling individuals to approach shifts with a composed, focused mindset. Accepting change as an inherent part of the professional tapestry propels us to adapt, evolve, and grow, rather than resist, deny, or panic when confronted with the unfamiliar.

6.2. Adjusting Your Perspective

Change can be regarded as a threat or an opportunity, depending on one's perspective. Pessimists, for instance, may view it as an unsettling destabilizer, threatening the equilibrium of their well-organised professional world. Optimists, contrarily, take it as an opportunity for growth and evolution, viewing every change as a chance to learn, explore, and push their boundaries.

Choosing the latter perspective isn't always easy, especially when the change is disruptive and arrives unanticipated. Nevertheless, reframing our mindset to perceive change as a catalyst for professional development and advancement leads to greater workforce resilience and adaptability, quintessential traits required for survival and success in a rapidly altering workplace.

6.3. Implementing a Growth Mindset

Having a growth mindset—the belief that skills and competencies can be developed through dedication and hard work—plays an integral role in this regard. Cultivating a growth mindset fosters the courage to take on challenges, the resilience to bounce back from setbacks, and the readiness to change habits and approaches in the face of change.

Establishing a growth mindset takes time, but it can be nurtured. Set small but achievable tasks to build your confidence and gradually increase the difficulty level. Use positive affirmation and visualization to boost your belief in your abilities. Critically evaluate your choices and make data-driven decisions. Above all, have a passion for learning and stay curious.

6.4. Enhancing Adaptability with Skill Development

Equipping yourself with a diverse skill set is a practical way of preparing for and adapting to change. Interdisciplinary know-how and transferable skills not only make you a valuable asset to any team but also provide a strong foundation when stepping into unfamiliar territories.

Continuous learning and development play a key role here. Training programs, workshops, courses, or seminars stimulate intellectual growth, provide insight into the latest industry trends, and enhance your professional network. Moreover, these initiatives instill confidence, reinforce adaptability, and make navigating the uncertain waters of change less intimidating.

6.5. Embracing Technological Shifts

Technology is a driving force behind workplace change today. As such, individuals who can quickly adapt to technological innovations, who are not scared to learn and apply new tools, are highly valued. Instead of being intimated by technological advancements, see them as opportunities to streamline work, increase efficiency, and create innovative offerings.

Develop your technological aptitude by taking online courses, reading up on tech trends, or simply playing around with new applications and software. Such practical exposure will enhance your technological fluency and prepare you for future uncertainty stemming from digital disruptions.

6.6. Flourishing through Change

Embracing change in the workplace does not entail enduring it passively. Rather, it is about harnessing its power, capitalizing on the opportunities it unveils, and flourishing, professionally and personally, amid shifting landscapes. It involves stepping out of one's comfort zone, overhauling outdated routines, learning new skills, and wrenching open the doors to experiential growth.

Change, however daunting, instigates transformation and progress. When we are open to change, proactive instead of reactive, and ready to adapt with agility, we reframe our professional story, charting an upward trajectory. Embracing change involves recognizing it, adjusting our perspective, fostering a growth mindset, continuously learning, and leveraging technological advancements to our advantage.

It takes courage to accept and adapt to change, but the rewards—improved skills, expansion of one's comfort zone, better resilience, and newfound perspectives—make the effort worthwhile. Remember, the only constant in life is change, and the ability to adapt is what determines success in our professional voyage.

Chapter 7. Professional Networking: Nurturing Connections in Your Field

The strength of your professional network can often become the operative factor behind some of your most significant career accomplishments. Relationships formed within your chosen field offer a wealth of opportunities and insights: broadened perspectives, insider knowledge, preferential involvement in projects, and a deep sense of camaraderie. Let's delve into the process, advantages, and ideal practices of professional networking.

7.1. Defining Professional Networking

Professional networking arises from constructive relationships established through career-related interactions with others, permitting shared-access to opportunities, knowledge, and resources. The vast professional landscape offers multiple platforms for networking, meetings or conferences, social platforms, corporate events, and even casual social interactions.

A network consists not only of individuals you connote as 'contacts' but also the people they know. This ripple effect of associations forms an interwoven mesh of professional relationships that empowers its members with an extended reach toward growth-related prospects.

7.2. Why is Professional Networking Vital?

A solid professional network can turn the tide in favor of your career ascent, offering a wealth of outcomes.

1. Speedy problem resolution: A thriving network could prove to be a fruitful resource for skill sharing and problem resolution, particularly when an outsider's input can positively transform your predicament.

2. New opportunities: Opportunities for jobs, collaborations, and special projects often come through established networks, creating pathways to professional development not otherwise available.

3. Personal growth: Networking encourages engagement with different perspectives, expanding your outlook and promoting enriching exchanges of work-related ideas.

4. Enhanced Reputation: Being an active part of a professional network also enhances your professional reputation, as others begin to view you as a resourceful, knowledgeable, and helpful individual.

5. Professional mentorship: Networks often harbor experienced professionals capable of providing guidance towards career advancement, enabling less experienced individuals to learn and grow.

7.3. Starting Your Networking Journey

A great place to start networking is within your current professional circle, but don't limit yourself to it. Attend industry conferences and events. Join webinars, online forums, and industry-specific communities. Use platforms such as LinkedIn, Twitter, or industry-specific social media platforms for online networking. Keep establishing connections without being arbitrary – selectivity in line with your career and professional goals is vital.

7.4. Building Meaningful Relationships

Networking goes beyond collecting business cards, a friend count on social media or arbitrary meet-and-greets. It's about nurturing relationships.

1. Be genuine: Authentic interest in others and building mutual connections fosters a strong network.

2. Offer help: Assist connections whenever possible. Shared victories instill a sense of camaraderie and create room for reciprocation.

3. Stay in touch: Nurtured relationships are enduring. Maintain contact and ensure regular communication with your connections.

4. Provide value: Offer pertinent advice, share helpful resources or provide introductions to other connections.

7.5. Elevating Your Networking Skills

Strategically expanding your network involves mastering vital networking skills.

1. Active Listening: Attentive interaction can reveal common interests and possible synergies and cultivates trust.

2. Relevant Engagement: Engage in discussions on contemporary industry trends and issues – sharing knowledge and expertise contributes to your reputation as a 'thought-leader'.

3. Balanced Interaction: Avoid hard-selling yourself. Aim for a genuine exchange of information and take the opportunity to learn from others.

4. Brand Presentation: Present your personal brand in a compelling and professional manner. Be articulate, clear, and confident.

7.6. Leveraging Your Network

Having a network is one thing; leveraging it to your advantage is another.

1. Skill Utilization: Leverage your network to seek advice, gain insight into industry trends, and learn about opportunities.

2. Be a connector: Introduce your connections to each other when relevant. This positions you as a valuable link within your network.

3. Engage in Reciprocity: Respect the reciprocal nature of networking. Be ready to return favors or help when your connections need it.

4. Promote diversity: Strive for a diverse network from different fields, positions, and organizations. This broadens your scope of opportunities and perspectives.

Proactive engagement in networking as a sustaining professional activity ensures that the inevitable ebbs and flows of your career do not derail your progress. The accumulated expertise, shared knowledge, access to resources, and allies that networking uncovers can invigorate your professional growth, thrusting you towards your ultimate career apex. Let the spark of networking be the beacon guiding your voyage through the thrilling choppy waves of career growth.

Chapter 8. The Growth Mindset: The Key to Endless Career Advancement

Human success stories are replete with instances of individuals who faced seemingly insurmountable odds, only to later triumph through their relentless persistence and adaptability. These are individuals with a specific mindset – the growth mindset. This concept, coined by psychologist Carol Dweck, posits that through hard work, tenacity, and consistent learning, people can grow and develop their abilities beyond initial expectations or limitations, resulting in endless career advancement.

8.1. The Concept of the Growth Mindset

The growth mindset is the belief that our most basic abilities can be developed through dedication, hard work, and love of learning. It contrasts with a fixed mindset, which holds that our traits are fixed, unchangeable, and that we are born with a certain degree of talent. Research reveals that the growth mindset creates a passion for learning rather than a hunger for approval. Hence, when faced with failure or hurdles, instead of feeling defeated, one sees them as opportunities for improvement, as food for growth.

8.2. The Impact of the Growth Mindset in the Workplace

The impact of the growth mindset goes beyond pure academics; it has profound implications in the workplace. Those with a growth mindset are more likely to view challenges as opportunities, to persevere in the face of setbacks, and to seek out feedback as a way to improve. This leads to higher productivity, greater creativity, improved problem-solving abilities, and better interpersonal relationships.

An experimental study conducted by Heslin, Latham & VandeWalle (2005) found that managers who were trained to adopt a growth mindset were more likely to notice improvement in their employees, provide coaching, and encourage employee development.

8.3. Cultivating a Growth Mindset

Cultivating a growth mindset is not a difficult task, but it necessitates consistent effort and attention. Here are some crucial steps to guide you:

1. Embrace challenges: Don't shy away from obstacles; embrace them. Challenges stretch you, and through them, you can unlock new potential.

2. Persist in the face of setbacks: Persevere when things get tough. It might be difficult to persist, but remember, the path to success is always under construction.

3. See effort as a path to mastery: Reframe the perception of effort. It's not just about getting things done; it's about mastering a skill or task.

Inculcating these elements in your work life may require deliberate practice, but the rewards are worthwhile.

8.4. Case Study: Microsoft's Growth Mindset Transformation

One of the most profound examples of a company-wide implementation of a growth mindset is by Microsoft under the leadership of Satya Nadella. When Nadella took on the role of CEO in 2014, he made it his mission to change the culture of the technology giant company to one of a growth mindset.

Through his influence, Microsoft moved away from a culture of know-it-alls to a culture of learn-it-alls. They broke away from the fear of failure, embraced challenges, and encouraged a collaborative learning environment. This transformation was key to their ability to innovate and grow in the competitive tech market.

8.5. Adopting the Growth Mindset for Endless Career Advancement

Advancing in your career and achieving your professional goals requires more than just skills and knowledge; it requires the willingness to learn, to adapt, and to grow. With a growth mindset, individuals become learners on a continuous journey.

It's important to acknowledge the effort behind success, view challenges as opportunities, and capitalize on feedback for improvement. When organizations foster a culture that supports the growth mindset, it can lead to better collaboration, innovation, and higher employee engagement, hence creating a vibrant and thriving workplace.

The growth mindset is an invaluable asset in modern work environments where change is the only constant. Cultivating and nurturing this mindset will ignite your career, facilitating steady upward mobility and a more fulfilling professional experience. When you embody the growth mindset, career advancement becomes a continuous journey of learning and growing. So, embrace growth, relish every challenge, and seek every opportunity to learn, for therein lies the key to unlocking endless career potential.

Chapter 9. Amping up Your Skillset: Lifelong Learning in Action

Learning stems from a perpetual desire to grow. Seeking knowledge and polishing skills is an ongoing endeavor, calling for commitment, curiosity, and resilience. Lifelong learning insinates an investment in personal evolution, geared towards enhancing employability, fostering innovation, and nurturing personal development.

9.1. Understanding Lifelong Learning

A concept tracing its roots back to ancient philosophers, lifelong learning embraces the pursuit of knowledge for personal and professional development. It necessitates a self-motivated commitment to learning - a continuous, voluntary and self-driven quest to acquire skills and understand novel concepts throughout life.

In a tumultuous business world, discontinuous learning is calamitous. New technologies, changing models of work, and the relentless call for innovation necessitate professionals to be lifelong learners. The COVID-19 pandemic, catalyzing a massive shift toward remote work and digital transition of business processes, further underscores this.

Lifelong learning is not confined to formal education or professional domains. It expands over various spheres, including personal breadths like health, relationships, hobbies, and mental resilience. It embarks on us an introspective journey, urging us to unlearn, learn, and relearn.

9.2. Lifelong Learning and Career Progress

Continual learning and strategic enhancement of skills sets bridges people with successful career trajectories. It is the cornerstone of professional growth:

- Augments Job Performance: Encyclopedic knowledge and varied skill-set leads to superior job performance.

- Enhances Employability: It boosts career opportunities by making professionals more adaptable and versatile in a rapidly evolving workspace.

- Boosts Innovation: An amalgamation of diverse insights, ideas, and knowledge fuels innovation.

- Fosters Resilience: Learning mindset prepares oneself for unpredictability and encourages adaptation.

- Cultivates Leadership: Continuous learning and development breed inspirational leaders who can manage and empower teams.

9.3. Devising Your Lifelong Learning Strategy

Creating a lifelong learning strategy requires introspection, planning, and commitment. Here, we explore a lucid, actionable approach for the same.

1) Identify Learning Goals: Sketch out your long-term professional and personal objectives and identify the skills and knowledge requisites for achieving them. 2) Seek Resources: Locate sources of learning that align with your goals - online platforms, webinars, podcasts, books, and mentors. 3) Create a Schedule: Integrate

learning into your daily schedule. Devote specific time blocks for learning activities. 4) Implement and Reflect: Apply the acquired knowledge and reflect upon results. It aids in understanding practical aspects and ensuring productive learning. 5) Review and Revise: Regularly revise your learning strategy, reflecting changing goals and requirements.

9.4. Gearing up for Action

Let's bring the lifelong learning strategy into activation. Here are some practices that can propel your journey:

- Read Regularly: Books provide comprehensive knowledge and insight. Develop a regular reading habit and explore various genres and topics.

- Leverage Online Resources: Use e-learning platforms and MOOCs. They provide flexibility, versatility, and extensive resources.

- Solicit Feedback and Mentorship: Seek feedback regularly. Mentorship can provide valuable insights, guidance, and support.

- Develop Curiosity: Promote critical thinking. Question, explore, and strive to understand.

- Attend Conferences and Seminars: These platforms not just increase learning, but also offer networking opportunities.

- Engage in Reflective Practices: Regular introspection about your learning process and results fosters self-awareness and ensures effective learning.

9.5. Lifelong Learning: Challenges and Countering Strategies

Though lifelong learning is beneficial, it may present challenges like time constraints, lack of motivation, or information overload. It's essential to have counter-strategies:

- Prioritize Learning: Adjust your schedule to prioritize learning. Remember, learning is an investment in your future.

- Create Learning Communities: Collaborate with like-minded individuals to encourage mutual learning, engagement, and motivation.

- Learn to Learn: Adapt to different methods of learning - active listening, note-taking, summarization, teaching others, or using flashcards.

- Embrace Failures: Understand that failures are integral to the learning process. They are stepping stones leading towards progress.

Lifelong learning is a commitment to self. It is a courageous endeavor to be in perpetual motion, to seek more, know more, and be more. Fuel your growth engine, keep your curiosity aflame, and remember - the journey of lifelong learning is just as critical as the destination. Embrace this journey and experience a professional and personal metamorphosis. The revitalizing adventure of continuous learning affirms the quintessential belief - You are always a work in progress.

Chapter 10. Professional Wellbeing: The Balance Between Career and Life

Finding equilibrium between your career and personal life isn't simply a worthy goal; it's essential for your physical, mental, and emotional wellbeing. Yet, in our dynamic, goal-oriented society, achieving this harmonious balance seems like an elusive quest. Let's explore how you can reclaim your professional health by striving for equilibrium, embracing flexibility, adopting mindfulness, setting boundaries, and trusting in the power of delegation and relaxation.

10.1. Achieving Equilibrium

An equilibrium in life doesn't denote a perfect 50/50 balance between your work and personal life, mainly because such purported perfection doesn't exist. It's about finding a happy medium that allows you to fulfill your work objectives without overlooking your personal ones.

This equilibrium remains fluid, often requiring consistent reassessments and adjustments. To find your ideal balance, consider the following principles:

1. Monitor Your Lifestyle: Ideally, your lifestyle should reflect your values and aspirations. Keep a record of how you spend your time. Spot patterns and imbalances that need adjustment and reassess your priorities.

2. Establish Realistic Goals: Determine what you want to achieve professionally and personally, then set feasible, measurable objectives.

3. Cultivate an Attitude of Acceptance: Accept that there will be

times when work demands more time, and times when personal life takes precedence. Acceptance eliminates guilt and reduces anxiety.

10.2. The Power of Flexibility

As you strive for equilibrium in your professional life, flexibility plays a crucial role. Embracing adaptability enables you to manage work-life challenges effectively.

Workplace flexibility might involve adjusting start and finish times, occasionally working from home, or compressing work hours. Such adjustments might seem insignificant, but they can enormously reduce personal stress, boost job satisfaction, increase productivity, and enhance overall wellbeing.

Adopt a proactive approach by discussing flexibility options with your employer, confirming the tasks you're expected to accomplish, and exploring the potential for tasks' reshuffling to accommodate your personal obligations.

10.3. Mindfulness and its Impact

Mindfulness refers to the mental state achieved by focusing your awareness on the present moment, calmly acknowledging and accepting your feelings, thoughts, and bodily sensations.

By practicing mindfulness, you can improve your focus and reduce stress and anxiety. This concept, when applied to professional wellbeing, facilitates emotional intelligence, improves decision-making abilities, and nurtures healthier interactions with colleagues.

Simple methods to adopt mindfulness at work include: 1. Start Your Day Without Stress: Complete your most challenging tasks early, leaving the rest of the day less stressful. 2. Mindful Breathing: A few minutes of focused breathing can recharge your mind during busy workdays. 3. Mindful Listening: Actively listening during interactions brings more clarity and understanding, reducing miscommunications and workplace conflicts.

10.4. Boundary Setting and Respect

Despite the interconnectedness of work and life, setting boundaries between them is essential. Precise boundaries help safeguard your time and foster respect for both professional and personal commitments.

Establish clear physical and temporal boundaries. Dedicate specific spaces for work, and set particular work hours to uphold work-life separation. Digital boundaries are equally crucial: designate screen-free time, avoid checking work emails during personal hours, and mute work-related notifications during non-working periods.

Realize that respecting your boundaries is as crucial as setting them. Prioritize your well-being and refrain from violating these boundaries unless under unavoidable circumstances.

10.5. The Art of Delegation and Letting Go

Delegation is a powerful tool for improving professional wellness and productivity. Through effective delegation, you distribute work responsibilities evenly, alleviate stress, enhance team bonding, and foster a growth environment.

Delegating tasks might seem challenging initially. Therefore, start small. Pass on routine tasks to competent teammates or employ automation technology to handle repetitive tasks. As you get comfortable with partial delegation, assign responsibilities that involve decision-making or critical thinking.

An integral part of the delegation exercise is moving past the urge to micro-manage every assignment. Accept that people might perform the task differently. As long as the outcomes align with the set objectives, the diversity in the process can indeed be an enriching experience.

10.6. Embrace Regular Downtime

Work-life balance isn't about working less; it's about working smart and integrating regular resting periods into your day. Planned and adequate downtime aids in mental rejuvenation, spurring creativity, enhancing productivity, and reducing the likelihood of burnout.

Maintain a regular sleep schedule, integrate exercise into your routine, engage in refreshing activities or hobbies, and schedule some quiet time for reflection or meditation.

10.7. Conclusion

Typically, professional wellbeing is about more than just the balance between career and life. It's a symphony of various elements — like acknowledgement of fluid equilibrium, adaptive flexibility, mindfulness, boundary setting, effective delegation, and embracing downtime. In orchestrating these factors, you can create a fulfilling work-life harmony that bolsters your professional health, allowing you to revitalize, recharge, and refocus with a renewed sense of vigour.

Remember, it's a continual process of refinement and alignment to match your evolving priorities and circumstances. Embrace the journey, and you'll discover that the path to professional wellbeing is just as rewarding as the destination.

Chapter 11. Envisioning the Future: Setting and Achieving Career Milestones

Developing a clear vision of your future career path is crucial for rekindling the spark in your work life. Refocusing your attention on the professional goals that you aim to achieve will provide you with newfound momentum and drive. It is important to realize that envisioning the future is not merely wishful thinking, but it's about plotting a course and setting milestones that will guide you to your desired destination.

11.1. Embrace the Power of Visualizing Your Career Success

Just as athletes often visualize making the winning shot or crossing the finish line ahead of their competitors, professionals can likewise harness the power of visualization to drive their career success. Studies show that mental imagery can stimulate the same brain regions as actual physical actions, resulting in increased motivation, confidence, and belief in your ability to achieve your career goals.

Picturing yourself in the future after having successfully achieved various career milestones is a potent tool for motivating yourself to take action. Using visualization effectively, however, requires clarity. Have a clear picture of what career success looks like to you. Is it standing at the helm of a global enterprise or perhaps running a small, but impactful non-profit? Is it achieving a balance between your professional and personal life or reaching the pinnacle of academic research? Once you have concretely defined what success means to you, use this picture as a compass to guide your actions and decisions.

11.2. Understanding the BIG and the SMALL Goals

One common pitfall in setting career goals is the tendency to focus solely on the 'Big Picture'. While having a long-term vision for your career is important, it is equally significant to recognize and set small, actionable milestones that will gradually lead you towards your ultimate goal.

The smaller goals act as stepping stones, and each step you take brings you closer to the big goal. These smaller, short-term goals are tangible, manageable targets that can give you a sense of accomplishment and momentum as you work towards the larger, long-term goal. They also provide an immediate focus that directs your day-to-day actions and decisions.

Remember, a journey of a thousand miles begins with a single step. It is these small steps, when consistently taken, that lead to monumental progress.

11.3. Crafting Your Career Roadmap: Setting Achievable Milestones

A career roadmap is a comprehensive plan that outlines the various stages or milestones of your career journey. When crafting your roadmap, think of it as a puzzle. The completed puzzle represents your ultimate career goal, while each piece represents a career milestone that you need to achieve to reach your goal. Here are some steps to guide you in developing your career roadmap:

1. Identify Your Final Destination: This is your ultimate career goal. Be as clear and specific as possible when defining what you hope

to achieve in the long run.

2. Evaluate Your Current Position: Assess your current skills, experiences, and competencies. Recognize your strengths and areas that need improvement.

3. Set Milestones: These are markers that denote significant stages in your journey towards your ultimate goal. Milestones can be tied to skill acquisition, completion of projects, or promotion to certain roles. They should be Specific, Measurable, Achievable, Relevant, and Time-bound (SMART).

4. Plan Action Steps: For each milestone, identify what you need to do to get there. These steps could involve undertaking further education, learning new skills, networking, or taking on new roles or assignments.

5. Review and Adjust: Regularly review your roadmap to gauge progress and make necessary adjustments. This ensures that you remain on course, even amid changing circumstances.

11.4. Stretch Your Potential: Achieving Your Career Milestones

Achieving the milestones you set will require dedication, discipline, and continued learning. Here, expanding your skillset is key. Proactively seek opportunities for growth at your workplace or in your industry. Enroll in professional courses, attend conferences, or volunteer to steer new projects. These experiences not only stretch your skills but also offer demonstrations of your achievements — the progress markers for your career milestones.

All these strategies combined will ensure that you chart a career path replete with exciting milestones, inspiring success, and continuous growth. Remember, career planning is a dynamic process that requires your engagement and active participation. Stay focused, stay driven, and power through. You are now equipped to define what future success looks like to you, and the steps you need to take to get there. The future is yours to shape! Ground it in reality, stretch the possibilities and set sail to make it happen.